W9-CNA-829

WRITE RIGHT!

SUBJECTS AND VERBS
with Your Neighbors

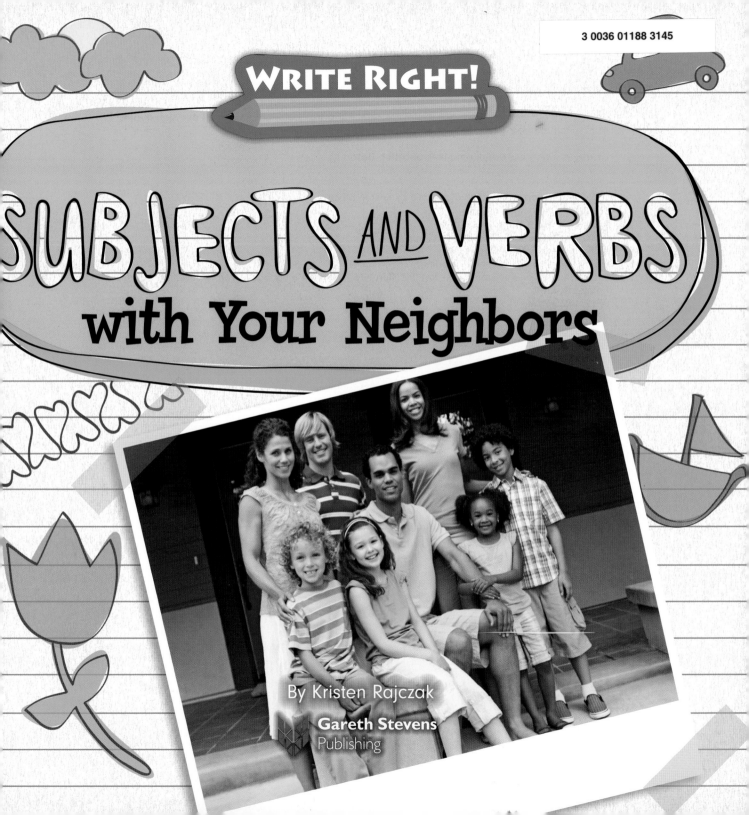

By Kristen Rajczak

Gareth Stevens
Publishing

Please visit our website, www.garethstevens.com. For a free color catalog of all our high-quality books, call toll free 1-800-542-2595 or fax 1-877-542-2596.

Library of Congress Cataloging-in-Publication Data

Rajczak, Kristen.
Subjects and verbs with your neighbors / by Kristen Rajczak.
  p. cm. — (Write right!)
Includes index.
ISBN 978-1-4339-9082-3 (pbk.)
ISBN 978-1-4339-9083-0 (6-pack)
ISBN 978-1-4339-9081-6 (library binding)
1. English language — Grammar — Juvenile literature. 2. English language — Verb — Juvenile literature.
I. Rajczak, Kristen. II. Title.
PE1271.R35 2014
428.2—d23

First Edition

Published in 2014 by
Gareth Stevens Publishing
111 East 14th Street, Suite 349
New York, NY 10003

Copyright © 2014 Gareth Stevens Publishing

Designer: Sarah Liddell
Editor: Kristen Rajczak

Photo credits: Cover, p. 1 Brand X Pictures/Thinkstock.com; pp. 5, 7 sonya etchison/Shutterstock.com; p. 9 © iStockphoto.com/CEFutcher; p. 11 Ghislain & Marie David de Lossy/The Image Bank/Getty Images; p. 13 Paul Bradbury/OJO Images/Getty Images; p. 15 (kids) Steve Dunwell/Photolibrary/ Getty Images; p. 15 (shovel) dabjola/Shutterstock.com; p. 17 © iStockphoto.com/kali9; p. 19 © iStockphoto.com/monkeybusinessimages.

Printed in the United States of America

CPSIA compliance information: Batch #CS13GS: For further information contact Gareth Stevens, New York, New York at 1-800-542-2595.

CONTENTS

From the Ground Up 4

And...Action!. 6

Make a Match 8

Only One "S" 10

Compound Subjects. 12

One or Another 14

Don't Come Between Us!. 16

Helping Out 18

Working Together. 20

Glossary. 22

For More Information. 23

Index 24

Words in the glossary appear in **bold** type the first time they are used in the text.

FROM THE GROUND UP

Sentences are the **foundations** of writing. A complete sentence starts with a capital letter and ends with a period (.), question mark (?), or exclamation point (!). It has both a subject and a verb.

The subject is the noun or pronoun doing the action of the sentence. A noun is a person, place, or thing. A pronoun is a word that stands in for a noun. *He*, *she*, *they*, *you*, *I*, and *we* are all pronouns.

ON THE WRITE TRACK

The subject of this sentence is highlighted: Tia walks around her small neighborhood. "Tia" is the noun doing the action.

The English language has many rules and **exceptions** to those rules. When trying to figure out if your sentence is written correctly, it's often helpful to say the sentence out loud. Many times, if it sounds right, it likely is.

AND...ACTION!

A verb is an action word. *Run, jump, eat*, and *forget* are all verbs. In a sentence, the verb tells the reader what the subject is doing.

Look again at the example from page 4:

Tia walks around her small neighborhood.

In order to find the verb, ask: What is Tia, the subject, doing in this sentence? Tia walks! Notice that together the subject and verb can be read as a complete sentence. That's a good way to check if the subject and verb are working together.

ON THE WRITE TRACK

A group of words that has a subject and a verb is called a clause. A clause that can stand on its own as a sentence is called independent.

MAKE A MATCH

When writing a sentence, you might take a while choosing what words to use. For example, adding **adjectives** and **adverbs** to a sentence helps show the reader what you are writing about. You have to choose the form of your words, too. Should they be singular or plural?

"Singular" means there's just one of something. "Plural" means more than one.

Both subjects and verbs can be written as singular or plural. But, whichever they are, the two must match.

ON THE WRITE TRACK

The matching of the "number" of a subject to the "number" of a verb is called subject-verb agreement.

When subjects and verbs agree, sentences are clearer.

9

ONLY ONE "S"

In most cases, when the subject of a sentence is singular, so is the verb.

A good neighbor helps those around him.

Similarly, a plural subject needs a plural verb.

Good neighbors help each other.

"Neighbors" is the plural of "neighbor." You can tell it's plural because it has an "s" at the end. In general, a sentence's subject and verb only have one "s" to share. Either the plural subject or the singular verb will end in "s."

Collective nouns—such as team and group—seem to **refer** to many people, but since the words themselves are singular, they commonly take a singular verb.

11

COMPOUND SUBJECTS

What if a sentence has more than one noun or pronoun in its subject? When the nouns or pronouns in a compound subject are joined by *and*, a plural verb should follow. The nouns in the subject may be singular or plural.

Melanie and Mrs. Bea bake bread together.

Ava, Miguel, and I climb the big tree at the end of the street.

Lexi and her parents choose the decorations for the cookout each year.

ON THE WRITE TRACK

In sentences that start with *here is* and *there is*, the subject comes after the verb. So, the verb should agree with what comes after it: There are five girls in the neighborhood who play on the soccer team.

Choosing verb **tense** is another part of sentence building. Tense tells whether the action will happen in the future, is happening right now, or happened in the past.

13

ONE OR ANOTHER

Sometimes, the nouns or pronouns in a compound subject are joined by *or*. If all parts of the compound subject are singular, then they take a singular verb.

Ms. Paula or Trina usually walks their family dog.

However, a compound subject that combines a singular and a plural noun with *or* is followed by a verb that agrees with the closest noun in the subject.

Louise or her friends shovel the sidewalk when it snows.

Shovel agrees with friends because it's the closer subject.

ON THE WRITE TRACK

Look at an example using two plural nouns: The Petersons or the Jacksons own a grill we can use to cook dinner. Own agrees with Jacksons since it's the closer noun!

Using or means there is a choice between two or more items.

15

DON'T COME BETWEEN US!

Subject-verb agreement rules don't change when **phrases** come between the subject and verb! But it's important to make sure the phrases aren't causing agreement problems.

> **Samari and Tamara**, who have been neighbors for years, **share** many garden tools.

Read the sentence without the phrase between the commas to see if it still makes sense.

> **Samari and Tamara share** many garden tools.

It does! The subject and verb agree.

ON THE WRITE TRACK

Most **indefinite** pronouns like *no one*, *anybody*, and *everybody* are considered singular, so they take a singular verb: Everybody on the street helps clean up after a windstorm.

The indefinite pronouns *all* and *some* can cause agreement troubles. How do you know if the verb is singular or plural? See if the noun the pronoun refers to can be counted.

HELPING OUT

Like main verbs, helping verbs must agree with the subject. The three main helping verbs are *be*, *have*, and *do*. They're often used with main verbs in the past tense. Helping verbs follow the same rules as main verbs in most cases.

Jack and Kate moved in last week. They don't know many of their neighbors.

Lucille learns about bird watching from Mr. O'Brien. He has lived a few houses down from her since she was a little girl.

ON THE WRITE TRACK

In sentences that have *neither* or *either* as the subject, the verb is singular.

When most verbs are used in the past tense without a helping verb, there's only one form that is used with both singular and plural subjects. It often ends in "-ed."

SOLD

19

WORKING TOGETHER

There are many rules when trying to make subjects and verbs agree. But since you use them all the time when you speak, writing a story with correct agreement is easier than you think. In the following paragraph, the subject-verb agreement is highlighted.

Everyone on the street **comes** to the summer cookout. This year, **the Petersons have offered** to have it in their backyard. The **food**, of which there's a lot, **is** always good! **Mr. Fine and Paul bring** hamburgers. **Either Denise or Ms. Gia makes** coleslaw.

ON THE WRITE TRACK

Here's another exception! The pronouns *you* and *I* take a plural verb.

REVIEWING SUBJECT-VERB AGREEMENT

rule	example
singular subject means a singular verb	Paul eats a donut.
plural subject means a plural verb	Dogs run quickly.
compound subjects joined by *and* have a plural verb	Gerald and Elise own a boat.
compound subjects joined by *or* have a verb that agrees with the closest subject	My brother or my parents find the best presents.
collective nouns use a singular verb	The team wins every game.
helping verbs follow agreement rules	Patrice has tried every cookie they make.

GLOSSARY

adjective: a word that describes a noun or pronoun

adverb: a word that describes a verb

exception: a case to which a rule doesn't apply

foundation: the support upon which something rests

indefinite: not limited

phrase: a group of words

refer: to direct attention to

tense: the form of a verb that tells the time of the action

FOR MORE INFORMATION

BOOKS

Hall, Pamela. *Wheel of Subject-Verb Agreement.* Edina, MN: Magic Wagon, 2009.

Riggs, Ann. *Verbs and Adverbs.* Mankato, MN: Creative Education, 2012.

WEBSITES

Scholastic Homework Hub: Grammar
www.scholastic.com/kids/homework/grammar.htm
Review the many different parts of speech.

Quiz on Subject-Verb Agreement
grammar.ccc.commnet.edu/grammar/cgi-shl/quiz.pl/sv_agr_quiz.htm
Test your knowledge with this online quiz.

INDEX

adjectives 8

adverbs 8

clause 6

collective nouns 11, 21

complete sentence 4, 6

compound subject 12, 14, 21

exceptions 5, 20

helping verbs 18, 19, 21

indefinite pronouns 16, 17

independent clause 6

noun 4, 12, 14, 17

phrases 16

plural 8, 10, 12, 14, 17, 19, 20, 21

predicate 7

pronoun 4, 12, 14, 17, 20

rules 5, 20, 21

singular 8, 10, 11, 12, 14, 16, 17, 18, 19, 21

subject-verb agreement 8, 12, 14, 16, 18, 20, 21

verb tense 13, 18, 19